MEET THE CONDITIONS

by

Robert Lee Horttor

Copyright 2009 Robert Lee Horttor

All rights reserved

ESBN: 1442177039

EAN-13: 9781442177031

Forward

Every man who walks this planet casts a shadow – a shadow of influence that affects those around him. Sometimes for good. Sometimes for bad.

This book reflects the shadow cast by a man who came to know the grace of God and learned to live life through the prism of that grace. With candor, Bob shares events and experiences, reflections of ministry and people he's met – real happenings taken out of real life.

Bob's story, both the humorous and serious parts will bless you. Too, you will see how God can use an individual who yields to Him.

Bob Horttor is a musician, a song writer, a witness for Christ, and a preacher of the Gospel. It is a privilege for me to know this man – both as his pastor, and co-laborer with him, but most of all, as his friend.

Blessed reading!

David Albright
Alive Center

Acknowledgments

Every Sunday School Teacher, every pastor, every class mate, every fellow worshiper and even the folk that had the authority to discharge me have had an influence on me and helped to shape my character. I thank you and the many others, not included in this book, who have added to my understanding. To each of you I am grateful.

My beautiful wife, Willie, endured much in our early years of marriage. As James said in chapter one verse seventeen "Every good gift and every perfect gift is from above, and commeth down from the FATHER of lights, with whom is no variableness, neither shadow of turning." I thank GOD for Willie.

Charlane Stear, Esq. graciously proof read the book. I cannot properly express my gratitude for that assistance. Every chapter had changes that needed to be made. A few places a rewrite was required to clarify the thought conveyed in the paragraph. **THANK YOU.**

Chapter 1

In the spring of 1968 I started to share a dream with a male relative. He stopped me and told me his dream. I was so taken with his worldly dream that I could not remember my dream. As spring turned into summer my dream was repeated. It was simply me pushing a loose tooth with my tongue until it was horizontal. In the summer, after the picture faded, the sound came on and said "Ye must become like a little child." With the summer dream came the knowledge that I had been given a warning and the knowledge that "Ye must become like a little child" was in the Bible. I started reading a few verses each evening as we were retiring for the night. You guessed it, I started at Genesis 1:1, just as a child would. Prior to making the decision to read the Bible, it would take between one-half hour to two hours for me to drop off to sleep. When the reading was established, it was difficult to remain awake for even a few chapters.

In the late 50's and early 60's, it was common practice for my wife and I to try to find technical books at second hand book stores. On some of these trips, we had bought a couple of second hand Bibles and I began to read from one of them. Although I didn't know it at the time, one of the children became curious enough about my reading material to discover that there were several places in the Bible where a page or two was missing. He was so concerned that he asked his mother "What will Daddy do when he gets to the place where the pages are missing?" When the time came that I found the first missing page, I got out the other 25 cent Bible and read the missing portion from that translation then returned to reading in the original one. That was not at all the reaction my family had expected.

After a year or two of daily Bible reading, I started wanting to go to church and since it had been my custom to sneak out of the house, I continued doing so when I finally started going to church. My first venture into church as an adult was to a church of the denomination that I attended for perhaps two or three years when I was early grade school age. When I left after the service was over, I felt as if I had intruded into a place where I was not really welcome. In the meantime, a lady had given me a two year subscription to VOICE magazine, published by Full Gospel Business Men's Fellowship, International. With the book of ACTS and First Corinthians fresh on my mind, along with VOICE magazine's many testimonies, I became hungry for the baptism of the HOLY GHOST. My second trip was to a Pentecostal church with a Sunday school total board which indicated the record attendance of twenty nine. This time there was no doubt that anyone seeking the LORD was welcome. One example of this is the night a drunk came in off the street and the service turned into the entire congregation ministering to him around the altar. Before the evening was over, that young man had received JESUS as his SAVIOUR. I started going on Sunday mornings, then on Sunday evenings. When Willie, my wife, started taking a night school class, I started going Tuesday evenings but I was sure to leave the service in time to be home before Willie got there.

The more I attended that little church and saw their concern for souls, love of the LORD, and liberty in the gifts of the SPIRIT; the hungrier I became to operate in the gifts of the SPIRIT. It was during this time that I claimed the promise found in Acts 2:38 "... Repent and be baptized in the name of JESUS CHRIST for the remission of sins, and ye **shall** receive the gift of the HOLY GHOST." The little church did not have a baptistery so I tried for several weeks to get someone to go to the river with me, for that purpose.

Tuesday evenings early enough to be through with it by the time Willie was out of class. By November, 1970, friends had agreed to let me use their swimming pool for that purpose. An appointment was made with them and with Bill Welch, my Sunday School Teacher. The day of my appointment, my friend had drained, cleaned and refilled the pool, so I expected the water to be very cold. Such was not the case. The water was very comfortable. My teacher baptized me "In the name of JESUS to the glory of the FATHER, the SON and the HOLY GHOST." I knew I had the promise but I continued to seek HIM in my prayers.

About this time a "big name" from down south was going to come to a church on the East side of town for a "HOLY SPIRIT" meeting. Another friend, John Bolinger, attended that church and asked me to attend with him because he knew I was seeking. The meeting started on Monday and was to continue each evening for that week. The first evening the "name" said that JESUS would appear in a vision on the podium the height of the building on one of the evenings before the meetings were to be over, and everyone there would see the vision. Because I wanted to see the vision, I **would not** miss a meeting. One evening the evangelist invited all who wanted to receive the HOLY SPIRIT to come forward for prayer. Lined up side by side were about twenty of us with me about one-fourth of the way from the left end. The evangelist started at the right end and spent about fifteen or twenty seconds with each person in the line. Without fail each person was "slain in the spirit", when he got to me, he placed his hand on my forehead, prayed then **pushed** me. I did not resist and the workers behind me let me gently to the floor. The end of the week came without me seeing or hearing anyone say they had seen the vision.

By the late spring of 1970, my mother-in-law could see that I had turned from the beer can to the BIBLE and bought a new BIBLE for my birthday. Could it be that mothers-in-law can detect changes in a man before his wife can? It must be difficult for a wife to believe that he won't revert to his old ways.

Chapter 2

One Man at the church promised five dollars to children who memorize the books of the BIBLE. Next Sunday one child had memorized them and received five dollars from the man. On the following Sunday another child had memorized them and received five dollars from the man, who at that time said that the promise had only been for the previous week. I was ashamed to be associated with people that make promises to children and then don't keep them. (Perhaps the reason I was so critical, was that had been one of my faults.) On several occasions I was tempted to tell the man. Each time I was about ready to speak, I would thumb the pages of my BIBLE and it would open to II Timothy 2:24 "and the servant of the LORD must not strive; but be gentle unto all men, apt to teach, patient." However, my desire to disassociate was so strong that I prayed if I should change congregations. One night, after the prayer, in a dream, his vehicle was going away with curses coming from the drivers window. Shortly afterwards, that man moved out of town.

The lady pastor, Ruby Eastwood, asked me to teach the Sunday School Class of children who were just turning into teens. I declined because I was not "filled with the SPIRIT" but she persuaded me that was not necessary so I took the class.

About every other Sunday evening I would be at the altar begging GOD for my family. One of these Sundays there was a message, I don't remember if it was a prophecy or an interpretation, "You have put that on the altar, leave it there, I will do the work." Another time there was a prophesy, "If Bob will give me a five day fast, I will do a great work." When I got home, I took a drink of water, noted the time of day and began the fast. By Friday afternoon I had lost twenty pounds. When I broke the fast at the Friday afternoon break at work, I was only able to hold two or three ounces of corn chips and one-half a soda. Ten pounds were put back on when the fluids were replaced in my body.

For portions of 1971 through 1973 Jerry, our oldest son, was working at the fire station in Richgrove. On one of our trips to see him, we were northeast bound on the old Famosa Porterville Highway when a man in a white Ford pickup ran the stop sign just as we were nearing the intersection and were to close to stop. I pushed on the brakes, the noise from that caused the man in the pickup to straddle the white line. I was headed straight to avoid rolling the car by moving the steering wheel. Just then the wheel jerked to the right in my hand and the car went into a skid, sliding to the left, then the wheel jerked to the left and the car skidded to the right partially onto the dirt shoulder of the road. The car was then lined up to go straight ahead to the right of the pickup. After we passed the pickup without touching, I pulled the car back into the roadway, waved at the man, and went on the way praising GOD.

One morning I was brushing my teeth and hit an exposed nerve in one of two cavities, I said a short prayer. Each of the cavities was large enough for me to hook a fingernail on. A few days later I was trying to find the cavity which I had felt while brushing but there was no sign of it although the other one was still there.

During this time I was underlining passages of scripture that made an unusual impression on me. Among them were Deuteronomy 30:6 "And the LORD thy GOD will circumcise thine heart, and the heart of thy seed, to love the LORD thy GOD with all thine heart, and with all thy soul, that thou mayest live," and the latter part of verse 19 "..therefore choose life, that both thou and thy seed may live:"; Ecclesiastes 2:24 "There is nothing better for a man, that he should eat and drink, and that he should make his soul enjoy good in his labor. This also I saw, that it was from the hand of GOD."; and Isaiah 3:10&11 "Say to the righteous, that it shall be well with him: for they shall eat the fruit of their doings. Woe to the wicked, it shall be ill with him: for the reward of his hands shall be given him."; Ezekiel 14:13 "Son of man, when the land sinneth against me by trespassing grievously, then will I stretch out my hand upon it, and will break the staff of bread thereof, and will send famine upon it, and will cut off man and beast from it." I believe Nahum was describing a vision of our automobiles in action when he penned Chapter 2 verse 4 "The chariots shall rage in the streets, they shall justle one against another in the broad ways: they shall seem like torches, they shall run like the lightnings." Another verse was Ephesians 5:18 "And be not drunk with wine, wherein is excess, but be filled with the SPIRIT."

On Sunday night October 21, 1973, there was a special moving of the HOLY SPIRIT. People were going to and from the altar, each with his own petition. I went to the altar to praise the LORD and when there were not enough words to properly praise HIM, I began praising HIM in tongues. I made several trips that night, over the course of about two hours, in order to become established so Satan would not be able to steal that promise from me.

8

Chapter 3

In the fall semester of 1972, I began a class in the Hebrew language at Bakersfield College. There was a time, perhaps as much as five years before beginning to read the BIBLE, when I saw a record album designed for the purpose of teaching Hebrew and almost bought it at that time. About the time of starting Hebrew studies, the LORD was showing me scriptures about being a watchman to Israel such as Ezekiel 33:3-6 "If he seeth the sword come upon the land, he blow the trumpet and warn the people; then whosoever heareth the sound of the trumpet, and taketh not warning; If the sword come, and take him away, his blood shall be upon his own head. He heard the sound of the trumpet, and took not warning; his blood shall be upon him. But he that taketh warning shall deliver his soul. But if the watchman see the sword come, and blow not the trumpet, and the people be not warned; If the sword come, and take away any person from among them, he is taken away in his iniquity; but his blood will I require at the watchman's hand." Ezekiel 33:11 "I have no pleasure in the death of the wicked; but that the wicked turn from his way and live: turn ye, turn ye from your evil ways: for why will ye die, oh house of Israel?", and Ezekiel 34:11-14 "For thus sayeth the LORD GOD; Behold, I, even I, will both search my sheep and seek them out. As a shepherd seeketh out his flock in the day that he is among his sheep that are scattered; so will I seek out my sheep, and will deliver them out of all places where they have been scattered in the cloudy and dark day. And I will bring them out from the people, and gather them from the countries, and will bring them to their own land, and feed them upon the mountains of Israel by the rivers, and in the inhabited places of the country. I will feed them in a good pasture, and upon the high mountains of Israel shall their fold be: There shall they lie in a good fold, and in a fat pasture shall they feed upon the mountains of Israel."

Because I parked on the street and my instructor, Rabbi Stanley Robin, was parked on campus he kindly offered me a ride to my pickup. When he pulled up behind it he saw the bumper sticker. It was the word JESUS in the frame color with the background only printed. He said, "My wife can read that but I can't." Years later Rabbi Robin helped me work out the Hebrew for "The Root Of David Has Prevailed" to place around the Star Of David for the cover of my first gospel song sheet music. On that same cover I showed an open book with the short form for life in Hebrew on the spline.

In the early 1970's I took a job with with a local agency at a rate of pay much less than what they paid their main line employees just out of high school. Even after a couple of raises my salary was very low. In February, 1974, there was a job opening with an engineering firm to oversee the construction of facilities for a new water district. At the new job, the salary was in line with the responsibilities. The salary was fifty percent above my old salary.

The engineering firm arranged for out of town attendance of a seminar which required overnight stays on two weekends. Willie was apprehensive about staying by herself at the motel while I was at the seminar. By the time of our second trip she had borrowed "protection." The following week included the first payday. Sunday morning I took the checkbook to church with me and, without consulting Willie, paid my first tithe. In the middle of the afternoon Willie was looking at the checkbook and discovered what I had done. She was very upset because I had given "her money to that woman" (the pastor). She told me, "If you don't get out of my house I'll kill you." Knowing the "protection" had not been returned, I loaded some clothes in the company car and found a motel room to rent.

A revival was "booked" for the church. When I arrived, I was told the evangelist did not show up and the members had, instead, started a painting project in the main room. The crew was using rollers with long handles to reach the high ceiling. The ceiling panels had grooves which the rollers would not cover. There was a ladder there which I took, with a gallon can half filled with paint, and began to paint the grooves. Willie came in and because my back was toward the door I was unaware of her approach. She pushed the ladder out from under me and I came to the floor and landed on my feet without even spilling any of the paint.

When our semimonthly payday arrived, I cashed the check and took one-half the take home pay by the house and gave to Willie. With the balance I paid tithes on the gross and lived on the remainder. Later that week, while I was in a service, Willie sent a friend in to give me a message that she wanted to talk to me. The friend took the family car back to the house while Willie and I went to the parking lot at the park to talk. Willie said, "I can't live without you" but she was not willing to agree to paying tithes and attending church until it became apparent to her that I was not coming back until she did. After her reluctant agreement, we then went to my motel room together to get my clothes and return home. I had agreed to let Willie select which church we would attend.

Chapter 4

We went to a few different churches and finally settled in at Sunshine Full Gospel Church. The couple teaching the four year olds left for the summer and the pastor asked me to teach that class just for the summer. I agreed but when the other teachers returned they declined the class. I continued teaching the class.

My work with the engineering firm continued until about October and I was again out of work. Unemployed for three months and desperate, I accepted a job with The City of Pismo Beach, starting January, 1975. While at Pismo Beach, I dreamed of a large field packed by foot traffic, surrounded by an eight foot high chain link fence. In that field, with Willie on my right with her left hand resting in my right elbow, we met a black haired, dark complexioned man with a black mustache. I spoke to the man in tongues. Later in the dream the man came up to Willie and me and began to speak to me in the language which I had spoken. We talked back and forth in that language without me understanding anything except that GOD was working. As I talked tears ran down the cheeks of the man. When I told Willie about the dream, she replied
"That's the way tongues are supposed to work." Another couple of thoughts came to mind while at Pismo Beach: one "ten thousand times ten thousand" and two "seventy foot boat." I did not understand either of these at that time. There was an instruction found in Psalms 81:10 "Open wide your mouth and I will fill it." April 6, 1975, Ezekiel 36:25, 26 and 29, "Then will I sprinkle clean water upon you and you shall be clean: from all your filthiness, and from all your idols, will I cleanse you. A new heart also will I give you, and a new SPIRIT will I put within you. ... I will call for the corn and increase it."

14

Willie and I were attending the Grover City Church of The Nazarene, where Larry and Sandy Pitcher were the pastors. At the beginning of the Pacific Ocean fishing season Travis, a commercial fisherman, invited the men of the church to his boat for an early morning fishing trip. The plan was to meet at church, go to Denny's for breakfast, and after that go fishing. Willie had gone back to Bakersfield for the weekend. Friday night, before the trip, I was reading scripture and came to "Sanctify ye a fast." As I started to read on, my eyes were drawn back to that phrase thirteen times before I was able to continue. In the next chapter there was this "sanctify a fast", my eyes were drawn back to that phrase about half a dozen times before I could continue. After I finished my routine reading I was earnestly seeking direction from the LORD. I asked for this sign. If they skip breakfast and go directly to the boat I will start the fast now, If they eat breakfast I will start the fast later. I packed a lunch just in case. When we met at the church one man said if we go now we can fish longer. A gruff voice from the rear said if I had known we were not going to breakfast, I would have eaten at home. We had breakfast at Denny's then went fishing. We had a good catch and ate lunch on board. I was not a fish lover in those days and was going to give my catch away. A young man told me to bring water to boil, put the fish in the water then turn off the fire and let the fish cook fifteen minutes while making a butter and garlic sauce, then I would like the fish. I tried that and when I picked up the pan and as I turned to pour off the water I heard this VOICE which said, "Go in the strength of this food three days." I began the fast after that meal.

As summer neared, Willie began spending time with our two sons still at home in Bakersfield. One was in his senior year of high school and the other was in college. I would catch the bus home and back to Pismo on weekends. One Sunday afternoon on the return trip I was reading a book by Don

Basham entitled FACE UP WITH A MIRACLE. He was telling about ministering the HOLY GHOST to a young man from his church and prophesied to him. A part of those words became so large the sentence covered both pages and and moved as if to have life in them. These are those words: "For I have not sent them out one by one but two by two a man and his wife to minister to my HOLY NAME."

Next door to the city hall there was a Catholic Church. One day I talked to a young priest and he told me there was a group of Charismatic Catholics that meet in the old church in Grover City on Thursday Nights. The first time I attended their meeting I was burdened for souls and was weeping in the SPIRIT. The entire group gathered around me and began to pray **softly** in the SPIRIT and after a few minutes I was laughing in the SPIRIT. I went to several other meetings and was always blessed when I went there.

I heard there was also a group meeting monthly in the basement of the mission in San Luis Obispo. There were about two hundred people at the meeting the evening that I went. Early in the meeting, the leader let a boy about eight years old talk about all the places he had walked in the last month. The answer to the question that had formed in my mind (Why is he letting this child talk so much?) came when the leader told us that before the last meeting this child had not been able to walk. GOD had done a work then. Praise HIS NAME.

Gene Smith was one of the members at the Nazarene Church. He invited me to a Full Gospel Business Men's Fellowship meeting at Morro Bay. The next meeting we attended was at the Madonna Inn in San Luis Obispo. I gave part of my testimony. The main speaker shared how he had been part of the mob but was now sharing the gospel. The report was that people do not get out of the mob alive in normal circumstances. GOD had again moved in a convert's life.

Mr. Francis, owner of James G. Francis Contractor, Inc., offered me a job estimating and bookkeeping for slightly more than I was making in Pismo. It was a chance to return home and drop the expense of maintaining extra quarters. In the last week at the Pismo Beach job I led the janitor through the sinner's prayer, before work started, in the men's room where I had gone to prepare coffee. Eight and one half months seems like a very small amount of time to spend for an eternal soul.

We were bidding a paving job in the early 1980s. Mr. Francis had settled on an amount well over half million dollars. As he was leaving the office, he told me to look it over and "change it if you want to." After he was gone, I said a short prayer, was impressed to lower the bid by one thousand dollars. I finished the paper work and took it to the bid opening. When the county officials opened the bids we were low bidder by five hundred dollars. At the company Christmas party that year, Mr. Francis told the entire crew about that.

Chapter 5

Back in Bakersfield, I wrote to the FGBMI headquarters about starting a local chapter. They replied there was already a chapter in Bakersfield. The president of the chapter was David Cotta and the vice president was Jerry Todd. They included contact information. My most memorable meeting was the one when Errol Shaw, Esquire came to me and said GOD had told him if he would have me pray for him, his back would be healed. He pulled up a chair, kicked off his boots and lifted his feet until his legs were horizontal. I kneeled, grabbed his ankles in my palms, **tightly closed my eyes** and prayed in the SPIRIT. About eight years later a choral group from his church was ministering at my home church. Mr. Shaw gave his testimony about that day and said that he had not had back problems since. Because of Mr. Shaw's faith and obedience, GOD had healed another one, Praise HIS NAME.

In 1977 Mike Esses was the speaker at one of the meetings and he gave me Isaiah 43:2 "When thou passeth through the waters, I will be with thee; and through the rivers, they shall not overflow thee: when thou walkest through the fire, thou shall not be burned; neither shall the flame kindle upon thee." Then on February 4, 1978, when Mark Willhite was ministering, he gave me Isaiah 43:18&19 "Remember ye not the former things, neither consider the things of old. Behold, I will do a new thing; now shall it spring forth; shall ye not know it? I will even make a way in the wilderness, and rivers in the desert." Then there was the time in 1976 or 1977 that Ed Gary pointed me to I John 2:27, "But the anointing which ye have received of HIM that abideth in you, and ye need not that any man teach you: but as the same anointing teacheth you all things, and is truth, and is no lie, and even as it hath taught you, ye shall abide in HIM."

18

It was around this time that Willie, Dad and I went to Tacoma to visit my brother Jack. While we were there Jack and I went to a luncheon meeting of the Tacoma Chapter of FGBMFI. While we were there I asked the president of the chapter when they were going to have a dinner meeting. He told me there was one scheduled for that evening. I went to the evening meeting alone because Jack had to work that shift. Because I was from out of town, the president asked me to speak to the group. As I was sharing my heart with them, I spoke one sentence in tongues. The meeting continued and after dinner a lady ran over to me and asked me to speak to a gentleman who was a friend of their family they had invited to the meeting. She told me the gentleman knew the language I had spoken in tongues. Not wanting to force myself on him I would not go over. Finally her husband and the man came to where I was. The gentleman told me that during the Korean War he was an officer on a ship in the Western Pacific and he recognized the language as Tagalogic. I had never heard of that. He explained that it was spoken in the Philippines.

October 13, 1978, the LORD quickened to me Jeremiah 30:2 "This speaketh the LORD GOD of Israel, saying, Write thee all the words that I have spoken unto thee in a book." Summer 1977, Proverbs 24:27, "Prepare thy work without, and make it fit for thyself in the field; and afterwards build thine house." August 14, 1978, from the Restoration of the Original Sacred Name Bible, confirmed October 3, 1978 Haggai 1:8 "Ascend the mountain, and bring in wood and build the house; that I may be pleased therewith and get myself glory, saith YAHVAH." Haggai 2:4 part b "... and be strong all ye people of the land, urgeth YAHVAH, and work; for I am with you, declareth YAHVAH of hosts." I had underlined two verses in the same translation from Exodus chapter 23. Verse 20 "Lo I am sending a messenger before thee, to guard thee in the way, and to bring thee into the place which I have prepared," and verse 25, "So shall ye serve YAHVAH your ELOHIM, and HE will bless thy bread and thy water, and I will take away sickness out of thy midst."

In 1977 I was reading Revelation chapter five when I came across ten thousand times ten thousand (Second paragraph in chapter 4 in this book). I immediately thought HE (GOD) wants me to write a song about that. Before I was saved, I played the guitar and wrote a few country songs. After I was born again I put the guitar away for seven years because that had been such a part of my worldly life which I wanted to put behind me. I had started playing it again in 1975 after Gene Smith had convinced me that GOD could use that talent. I began writing a song, I multiplied 10,000 X 10,000 and came up with the name ONE HUNDRED MILLION, which I wrote at that time.

In the spring of 1980 while praising the LORD in the shower HE gave the words and music for a chorus. After I dressed I went into the living room and played the chorus on the piano until it was memorized. As I continued to sing it and worship I began to sing in tongues to the new tune and looked over my shoulder to see Willie standing in the hallway looking around the door facing at me. When I looked she left. I wrote the first verse that night but did not write other verses until Willie took her mother to Hobbs, New Mexico, to visit relatives. While she was there I wrote two other verses. In January 1981 I shared with Bob Clark about the LORD giving me the chorus. February 27, 1981, Mr. Clark came to the office and told me that he had a man who would play the keyboard without charge for a recording session and that he would do the engineering. And he might be able to get a bass player. He knew that I play the guitar and wanted a fiddle in the band. He said all the expense I would be out would be the the studio rental and whatever pay Jelly Sanders, one of my favorite fiddle players, would require. That song was from Matthew Chapter 26 which I called THIS CUP. I don't read music so I enlisted the aid of our music minister to transcribe those two songs. Larry Runnels wrote them out for me and then had his wife, Martha, play them back. She read and played the score, as we made adjustments, until it sounded right then I published those songs in 1982.

I wrote two more songs. By this time Mr. Runnels had gone to minister in another city. I talked to the new music minister and he agreed to do the work for me. I paid him up front but he never did any work on either of them although I had given him a tape of the songs. One song was named ASHAMED. When I had only one verse and the chorus written I shared that much with the men at a FGBMFI breakfast meeting at Hodel's in the Valley Plaza. After I sang what I had written an old gentleman prophesied "That song will be played on secular stations which will not play gospel music and will minister to many." The other song was entitled PASSOVER. One day I was driving and the adversary began to tell me about things I had done before I was saved. He was really trying to discourage me. The HOLY SPIRIT reminded me, that sin has been covered by the BLOOD OF THE LAMB. GOD had turned the attack back on Satan by having me write the song PASSOVER. It was 1989 before there was enough work done on the songs to register the copyrights.

On April 14, 1983, my youngest brother's birthday, I was moved to tears by a paid memorium on page A22 in the Bakersfield Californian. It was so moving that I had to read it twice. It was a tribute to Susan Michelle Binn who had gone to be with the LORD the preceding October. The memorium was 8 ½ inches wide and full page height. It included a photo of Susan 7 inches wide and slightly over 7 inches high. The letter to Susan from MOM was about her battle with leukemia and included, "You wrote a beautiful song to GOD" and concluded with these thoughts, "...thank GOD for kids...especially kids like you: and like the song says, because of kids there's magic for awhile, a certain kind of sunshine in a smile. Did you ever stop to think or wonder why, the nearest thing to heaven is a child?" and finally "Happy birthday, Susan! Happy birthday sweet sixteen!" then hand written

"Love, Mom"

After a couple of years I wrote to the Binns and asked about the song. October 1986 Mrs. Binn answered and graciously granted me permission to use the song as long as Susan got credit for it. In my memory it seems like it was originally called A LOVE SONG TO JESUS but I just call it SUSAN'S SONG. In the program for her services it was called JESUS, I KNOW YOU'RE UP THERE!

Chapter 6

January 3, 1979, our youngest son's wife, Sharon, was having problems with her pregnancy and was in Bakersfield Memorial Hospital. After a few hours I went to the chapel to pray. When I got up from prayer I looked at the open BIBLE there on a stand in the chapel. In the middle of the first column were the words "Sharon is like a wilderness." I looked at the other three columns and they all said essentially the same thing. GOD had shown me what was about to happen. Sharon miscarried. Days later at home I tried to find where there were four chapters that said what I had seen at the hospital. I could not do it. And still later I was back at the hospital and saw that the bible I had seen was four parallel translations. The scripture is found in Isaiah 33:9.

March 21, 1979, in the New American Standard and again October 15, 1979, in the New International Version I found "And Sharon shall be a fold of flocks." April 1980 Sharon gave birth to Melissa. PRAISE GOD. Thirteen months before Melissa was born, GOD had again shown me what was about to happen.

Just before Melissa was eleven years old, I was watching R. W. Schambach on TBN in the living room and when Melissa came into the room I changed the channel. She said "I wanted to watch that." I switched back and we watched the rest of the program. Near the end Rev. Schambach asked for a show of hands from those who wanted to receive Jesus as LORD. Melissa raised her hand and we both went and knelt in front of the TV. When the airing closed without praying I said, "He didn't pray." Melissa said "But, grandpa, I raised my hand." Then she told me she wanted to be baptized. After that she wanted to read from the BIBLE. She picked Matthew

Chapter 27. She read about ¼ chapter then she said it was my turn. I read about ¼ chapter, she read about ¼ chapter and I finished the chapter. Melissa said we will read Chapter 28 in the morning. Do you not know that GOD has said, "And a child shall lead them." This child had seen the HEART OF GOD better than grandpa had.

September 21, 1979, morning BIBLE reading at Proverbs 5:15 in the King James version then I checked the New International Version "Drink water from your own cistern, running water from your own well." Friday evening March 14, 1980, there was a chance meeting with George Davis at the Valley Plaza and he talked about the two of us joint bidding a job in Tehachapi, which would come up in the near future. On Saturday evening, March 15, 1980, I found a note with the preceding information on it. GOD STILL REIGNS. PRAISE HIS HOLY NAME.

About the last Sunday in January or the first Sunday in February, 1980, my Sunday School teacher, Juanita Essert, taught about a method for "an hour of prayer." At 2:00 am February 14, 1980, I woke with the word prayer very strongly impressed on my heart but not with a need for immediate prayer. In the morning Ken Copeland sang Sweet Hour of Prayer on his radio program and discussed the Victory after an hour of prayer and talked about intercessory prayer. The following morning he taught on congregational intercessory prayer. That was Friday. That evening, February 16, 1980, I stayed up until midnight building an altar. The next morning I finished nailing it together. When I showed it to Terry, our middle son, he only saw a bench.

Mrs. Essert's daughter, Donna White, came by the parcel of land where I was working one day on the way to see about her horse which was in need of healing. When she saw me she stopped to ask me to pray for her horse. As she went on, I began to pray and then realized I still had that old cowboy hat on my head. I threw the hat on the ground because the LORD reminded me of I Corinthians 11:4, "Every man praying or prophesying, having his head covered, dishonoureth his head." I continued to pray in the SPIRIT. We heard later, the horse was doing fine.

At the Oildale Assembly of GOD Sunday morning worship service June 8, 1980, there was a message in tongues. The interpretation was essentially as follows: I have set before you an open door. I have given you work to do, therefore work, be faithful and enter the open door. I have given you tools to work with, MY SPIRIT, understanding, MY WORD. I will give you fruit for your labor. The following Sunday as the class was assembling for Sunday School, I shared with those present my need for prayer to see the open door and Maudie McLoud said let's pray now (before class time) and those assembled gathered around and prayed for me. June 22, 1980, Sunday morning worship service, Pastor Marvin Kilgore delivered the following message. "GOD has everything ready for us. Have faith in GOD, follow HIM, and HE will bless you."

In the summer of 1976, Reverend Kilgore had a message from GOD that was "Ask what you will and it shall be given you." I went down to pray and asked GOD for all of the gifts and all <u>the fruits of the SPIRIT.</u> When I got up, I found that I was the only one who had gone to the altar but the rest of the people were standing quietly waiting on the LORD. With about 200 or more people in attendance, I thought the altars would be full.

January 20, 1979, FGBMFI breakfast meeting I requested prayer for Jerry's family and for myself. Russell Lusk, president at that time, exhorted those around to trust GOD in matters of the family, then spoke to me and said he knows that I do. Dave Smith was used to tell me that I have been forgiven but I do not have the joy I should have when I come before GOD.

In August 1980 Vonnie, my stepmother, went into the hospital for cancer surgery. They closed her up and told her to go home, there's nothing we can do for you. Willie and I went to visit her on Wednesday. While we were there she told Willie, **"I'm not ready."** It was then that my heart turned over in me. We went back on Saturday to visit and she was still in the hospital. I did not find a time to speak privately with her and did not feel led to say anything at that time. Willie and her mother had, for several weeks, been planning a trip to New Mexico to visit relatives. In the middle of the next week they left on that trip. The following Saturday I went to visit Dad and Vonnie. I went into the living room to visit Vonnie. She was lying on the couch which was against the North wall. There was an easy chair by the East wall, I sat there but could not face her because of the way she was positioned. I went into the kitchen, got a folding chair, sat it in the middle of the room, shared a few scriptures with her, then prayed for forgiveness of sins and for JESUS to come into her life. After we prayed she told me "**I'm ready now.**" It was about two weeks later that she went to be with the LORD. HIS timing is perfect. PRAISE HIS HOLY NAME.

December 11, 1981, In the late afternoon at the office I was having problems with my vision. At 5:43 the next morning the LORD led me to Isaiah 42:19, "Who is blind but my servant? or deaf as my messenger that I sent? who is blind as he that is perfect, and blind as the LORD's servant?" Oh the joy of GOD's moving!!

December 11, 1983, During the Sunday School prayer time Dola Hicks prophesied, "The promise to you I will keep. I love you as much as I love Abraham."

The office manager at work, Sue Machado, told me that at McKee Road Baptist Church it was the last night for the musical group known as June Wade and the Country Congregation to minister and asked me if Willie and I would like to attend. I asked her to call Willie and ask her. Willie agreed. After worshiping with the kind of music Willie and I really enjoy, Dale Wade gave his testimony. After that he asked for every head to bow and every eye to close and then asked for everyone who wanted to accept JESUS to raise their hand. I resisted the temptation to see if Willie had raised hers. Rev. Wade said I see those five hands, now you may look up. He then said, "Those of you who raised you hands come forward for prayer." Willie was the only one that went forward. GOD IS SO GOOD.

Chapter 7

1976 or 1977   from Berkley version Jeremiah 15: 13 & 19 ... 13 "Your wealth and your treasures will I give for spoil, without price, for all your sins throughout all your territory." ....19 "Therefore thus says the LORD: If you return, then will I restore you, and you shall stand before ME. If you bring out the precious from the worthless, you shall be MY mouth. They shall return to you but you shall not return to them,..."

Thursday morning February 5, 1981, I awoke at 3:33 a.m. went back to sleep and awoke again at 4:07 a.m. after dreaming. In the dream I saw the upper right corner of a yellow paper, which I took to be about 8 ½ by 11 inches in size, folded into 3 portions, about the size of a business letter. In the corner where a stamp would be placed were the hand written words:

Free
"Born again"

That evening at 9:54 p.m. I saw Ezekiel 36:27, "And I will put MY SPIRIT within you, and cause you to walk in MY statues, and ye shall keep MY judgments and do them."

Saturday February 21, 1981, Willie and I went to visit my dad. Dad's friend Otis was there. When I first went into the house I shared a few scriptures with Otis and then the conversation turned to things that interested Dad and Otis. After several minutes, Willie took her little dog out for a walk. While she was out, Otis said that he was going home, do the laundry, and then "go to hell." I quickly told him he didn't have to go there. I shared Romans 10:9, "If thou shall confess with thy mouth the LORD JESUS, and shall believe in thine heart that GOD hath raised HIM from the dead, thou shall be saved," with him, then prayed "LORD forgive us for our sins and come into our hearts." I said, "Amen," and stared at Otis, but when he did not respond I said "Amen" louder. I was surprised to hear Dad say "Amen" and then Otis also said "Amen." After visiting for a while, when Willie and I were leaving, Otis, still there, said, "You've got JESUS in your heart and now you've got HIM in mine." PRAISE GOD.

March 10, 1981, While waiting at the Getty Oil Co. Taft Office to meet a man I opened the New Testament at random to John 21: 16 & 17 where JESUS was telling Peter, "Feed MY sheep." After the meeting, while returning to Bakersfield, "Feed MY sheep" came strongly into mind so I began singing Peter, Feed MY sheep. Peter, Lovest thou ME? Yea, LORD; THOU knowest that I love THEE. Feed MY sheep. As I continued singing, it would not remain Peter but it became "Robert" Lovest thou ME? LORD, you know my heart better than I do. "Feed MY sheep."

March 29, 1981, Sunday evening Rick Smith prophesied, "You have the word in you ...Now you must begin to use it." Then in the morning service April 5, 1981, Prophesy from the platform, "My child, I have seen the question marks, I have seen thy tribulations...If thou will stand to thy feet to reaffirm thy faith I will......" I stood to worship in obedience to the prophesy. After a time, I looked around but found that I was the only one standing except those on the platform.

April 23, 1981, I began to consider what I should do in response to the teaching of CHRIST in the last eight verses of Mark Chapter 9 when I saw a faint overlay of shocks of grain superimposed on the things I was seeing with my natural eye. Next Sunday morning there was a prophesy. It said, "Hold to that which I have given you. Hold fast for, I say, I will come again. There is an adversary who will come. Hold fast to that confidence. For I say again, hold fast to that which I have given unto you."

November 29, 1981, GOD was moving throughout the congregation by HIS SPIRIT. The congregation was divided into groups ministering to each other. As the SPIRIT began to move on me, I began talking in tongues with my Bible open to the first chapter of Joshua. I walked up to Mark Brown and continued talking in that unknown tongue. A few years later, at another church, as Mark and I talked he told me that Reverend Kilgore had asked if he knew what I was saying. He said that he did and shared with me at that time what was being said was the third verse of chapter one of Joshua, "Every place that the sole of your foot shall tread upon, that have I given unto you, as I said unto Moses."

Sunday morning December 18, 1983, woke at 6:25 after this dream: In a living room filled with people, I was standing, most others were seated. Across the room to my left and at the end of the room to my right were two women (one at each location). Both were slightly stout and appeared to be from places other than America. While I was distracted there appeared a large menacing looking man whom I assumed had come in the front door. I began speaking in tongues to the women mentioned above, primarily to the one to my left but occasionally to the one to my right. At the end of the message, the lady on my right said, "This hood affects 50 people..." trailing off as if not completing the interpretation of the message which apparently was in the two ladies native tongue. At that point the large menacing man was no where in sight and not having seen him leave I looked in the kitchen and down the hallway. Because I did not see him I cried out in a loud voice "Come out in the NAME OF JESUS" Just then someone lying on the couch with a cover over him began to expel something from within, only then did we know where the menacing spirit had gone.

March 1986 The company I was working for was having trouble collecting subcontractor money owed them from prime contractors and laid me off. After a few weeks out of work, Willie insisted that I ask my cousin Doug Wegener for a job. Reluctantly, I went to his office and found that they were having trouble with the business and their health. I prayed with them and went away. A few days later I received the following letter from them. " March 30, 1986   Dear Robert,   Just wanted to take the opportunity to thank you, and tell you how much your visit to our office and your prayer for us has meant.   When you walked into our office on that morning, I know you thought you had come looking for a job. But I think God had something different in mind for you.   I am so thankful that your heart and mind are so open to the leadership of the Holy Spirit. Because as far as we are concerned he led you to the right place at the right time. The morning you came into our office I believe was one of the most difficult days of our lives. At that time it seemed like being dead would have been easier than facing what was ahead of us that day. We were faced with all the terrible emotions of ending a business we had worked so hard to build, plus fighting a physical battle with the flu.   We felt near the breaking point. Even though that God has promised that he will give no more than we can bear. And that he allows us trials in our lives so that he can bring us through them and make us strong in the end.   We were facing a meeting with the IRS that morning and a meeting with a representative from Shell Oil Company in the afternoon. The results of those two meetings was nothing short of a miracle from God. The IRS agent's attitude had changed from closing us down to what can we do to remedy the situation. Doug's meeting with Shell Oil Company and the result of that meeting was "What can we do to help?   We need good contractors, and don't want to loose you."   Here is the biggest miracle of all.   All of our contracts with Shell were changed from Net: 15 and Net: 30 to Net Immediately. We were Federal Expressed over $300,000 within three days. If getting an oil company to turn loose of that amount of money in that short of time isn't a miracle I don't know what is. Robert, you may not think of yourself as being in the ministry, but we certainly do because you surely ministered to us in our time of need. I also believe God used Willie in this, if she had not encouraged you to go job hunting maybe you wouldn't have come on that day when we needed your prayer so badly. I am not saying that everything is perfect but things have come a long way. I feel that God started our business with a miracle and he has kept it going with more than one miracle. I feel life is worth living and I even enjoy going to the office again. Robert, we pray that God will lead you in the decisions you are facing in your life. Thank you again for being open to his leadership. We love you! Doug and Beverly Wegener"

May 20, 1986, 1:00 a.m. Woke up, pulled a card from the box Re: I Corinthians 15:58, "Be steadfast, immovable, at all times aboundingly active in the LORD's service, aware that your labor in the LORD is not futile."

July 24, 1986, When I was in six year old Melissa's room as she was going to bed I asked her if she would like to pray. After she had thanked GOD for this day, she told me she didn't want to do Eddie's (her brother's) praise, so she said her own praise. At an earlier date I had told her "Just talk to GOD," in response to her statement "I don't know any prayers."

Saturday July 26, 1986, Eddie was at our house for the weekend. I called Reverend Kilgore and asked him if we could dedicate him to the LORD in tomorrow's service. He told me the schedule was full, but I pressed him because we rarely had Eddie over. He relented and on Sunday July 27, 1986, Willie and I dedicated Eddie to the LORD at the Oildale Assembly Of GOD Church with Reverend Kilgore ministering.

Thursday July 31, 1986, Around 5:30 or 5:45 p.m. Willie had prepared food for Melissa and little Ed while waiting for their dad to pick them up. Little Ed began to say "JESUS is coming again, JESUS is coming again, JESUS is coming again." He was four and one half years old at that time. GOD uses anyone who is obedient, including young children. Samuel was a child when GOD began to use him.

November 6, 1985, In the early morning I dreamed I was trying to cook pancakes on a grill through a small window on the back side of the grill. The grill had yellow cooking oil boiling on it and I was trying to to pour batter from a plastic bag. I was having trouble trying to turn the pancakes through the small window. As I continued trying to cook coaster sized pancakes, some other man on the front side cooked some stack sized pancakes and went on. I continued trying to cook mine and the dream ended as I was pouring <u>dry pancake mix</u> from the plastic bag I had been pouring batter from at the start of the dream. May 3, 1994, 10:34 p.m., while reading this record, it occurred to me that I cannot get anything useful done with my mix unless the anointing oil is blended with it. <u>I must have GOD in all of my activities.</u>

Chapter 8

October 30, 1986, Sometime between 4:47 a.m.and 4:53 a.m. I awoke after dreaming that I was sitting in the back seat of a car. Printed on the inside of the back window glass, over my head, in large bold black letters was the message... "GOD wants people who walk 97% of the time."I reread this note the evening of May 3, 1987, then the next day, just after lunch, I began to wonder about the meaning of the dream as I was taking a walk at the Cache Creek job. With an hour drive each way to and from the job, I figured I would have to walk for 66 2/3 hours on work days to make the percentages figure out. It occurred to me that in the pew I am riding but when I am ministering I am walking. GOD wants all of us to minister to others.

May 1, 1987, My hat blew off my head and started tumbling in the high wind at Cache Creek. I said, "In JESUS NAME." The hat sat down flat then slid about 1½ or 2 feet then stopped. I walked over and picked it up. The wind did not stop blowing but I thought about the time that JESUS calmed the water.

July 12, 1987, Prophecy after church through Mrs. Bill Welch: "My son you are a chosen vessel. You are troubled... stress ...fear. Satan will tempt you. Do not yield to him. I will shake you. Tonight you will have peace. I will shake you. I will lead you in a way that you have not considered. I will lead you in a clear path. You are a chosen vessel."

March 6, 1988, Before Sunday School, in the class room, Marilyn Danley told me this. Friday night she dreamed that I was praying in tongues. The LORD gave her an interpretation. She did not get up and write it down so the interpretation came several times in the night. In the morning she wrote it down. "My son, you are a mighty man. You are a conqueror. Hold fast onto the LORD. Even though you have had wounds, the LORD is your strength. Draw nigh unto the LORD so that your joy may be full."

April 17, 1988, Sunday evening Missionary Service by Gail Barber. At the altar, as the service was ending, I was very heavy and weeping in my spirit for souls. I would weep before the LORD, then pray with others, then return to weep before the LORD. Near the end of the altar service Troy Tennet began praying with me and brought this message. "Just as I told HEZEKIAH to put his house in order....even so I will add fifteen years to your life. I have seen your heart, I have seen your tears." April 19, 1988, I was grade checking for the firm of Larry D. Weese on a project West of Buttonwillow. I was intent on finishing a check, I looked up and saw the operator had turned sideways from the way he had been working and was backing toward me. The ripper bar on the back of the blade (known to others as a road grader) nearly hit me in the head before I was able to get out of the way.

April 25, 1988, Before Sunday School Tim Goolsby was showing Richard Goldberg and another young man a solid anointing mixture that contained Frankincense and Myrrh. The young men were touching and smelling the mixture. I started to do the same but said, "No, anoint me to do the work of the LORD." Tim did just that and the three young men prayed for me. After the morning worship service was over, Richard came to me and read Mark 16: 17 & 18 from the Amplified Bible. "And these attesting signs will accompany those who believe: in My name they will drive out demons; they will speak in new languages; They will pick up serpents; and [even] if they drink anything deadly, it will not hurt them; they will lay their hands on the sick, and they will get well."

July 17, 1988, A class member handed me a note dated 7-13-88 It said, "Robert - My son - I know the desires of your heart. But know that my ways are not your ways and my time is not your time. You will have your ministry – in due season – just have patience, my Son. And your wife, Willie, will be at your side, I have called you together from heaven and what God has put together, let no man take apart. Be patient, my Son. My desire is to give you your desires."

April 16, 1989, Sunday evening around 9:00 pm Willie received a call that my mother had fallen, was taken to Lindsay Hospital and was in intensive care. Willie had a doctor's appointment the following morning so we went to Lindsay after that. We came home Monday evening and went back to Lindsay Tuesday. Tuesday night we stayed at Mom's house. About daylight Wednesday morning Fred, my youngest brother, called to tell us the nurse had called the family to the hospital. When we arrived the doctor had told Fred and later told Willie, "He would be surprised if she made it through the day." By noon she was staring into space and talking to family members who had already gone into eternity. I was trying to make this side of her crossing easier. About 1:00 pm she was not responding to the nurses or to Willie and her eyes were rolled back. Willie came to get me off the phone to talk to Mom. She responded to my voice but was showing great agitation. At that time I began to stroke her brow and softly say, "Peace in JESUS NAME." After a couple of minutes of this mom then appeared peaceful. I began softly singing "There's peace in the NAME of the LORD." When Mom appeared to be in real peace, I began singing of other things in the NAME of the LORD and thought about healing but passed over that because I still thought it was the time for her crossing into eternity, but after I had sang one other thing then I felt compelled to return and sing, "There's healing in the NAME of the LORD." After that

I began singing other gospel songs and mom started singing with me. Mom began to improve. She left intensive care for a regular room on Saturday. Monday she left the hospital for her home in Plainview.

May 7, 1989, Sunday morning, Richard Goldberg said when we were worshiping this morning he saw light radiating from me even to outside the church building. When he asked GOD what it meant, GOD said, "His love and prayers for others is causing the gospel to be shed even beyond this building."

One day Richard handed me a sheet torn from a spiral binder. On it he had drawn a picture frame with Bob's picture of the ministry GOD has given him written under it. Next to that was the mathematical symbol for does not equal and then another drawing with GOD's Ministry for Bob written under that. Then this message, "Think not that there is a step yet to be taken. Now is the time. Today is the day you have been and are a servant and minister for ME and MY people. I will cause your ministry to continue to grow & grow & grow 1 by 1 by 1 by 1 !!!!"

May 10, 1989, New American Standard, Isaiah 33: 16, "....His water will be sure."

May 25, 1989, Dreamed about an earth moving job where I was the grade checker. Most of the earthwork was done with the original stakes still in place on mounds of dirt to save them. End of dream. It seems to me that the meaning is the work is almost complete with only a little time left for cleanup but the grade checker (that's me) has a lot of work to do in a short time in order for the job to be finished.

August 29, 1989, In the morning I wrote a chorus for a song called Build A Road. That evening I could not recall the tune. The next morning GOD brought the tune to remembrance. PRAISE HIS HOLY NAME. September 1, 1989, Psalm 57: 7b "...I will sing and make music."

Two more choruses were written within a year or two of BUILD A ROAD. They were TEMPLE and GIFTS. None of the verses were written until 2007.

February 18, 1990, After the evening service, I prayed for Richard Goldberg then he prayed for me. He said that the FATHER, not the SON, not the HOLY GHOST; was taking his time with a diamond cutter's bar and a wooden mallet and very carefully positioning the bar indicating that the LORD was working on me to have me become exactly what HE wanted me to be. November 16, 1990, NAS Isaiah 62:3b, "...You will...be..a royal diadem in the hard of your GOD."

June 9, 1990, 5:00 a.m. Saturday Psalm 102:28, "The children of thy servants shall continue and their seed shall be established before thee."

July 25, 1990, After evening service, part of message through Mrs. Bill Welch. These feet shall carry the gospel into many countries.... your wife will walk with you... you will notice a difference even tomorrow...Many more songs shall flow through you and will bless and bring many into the kingdom. You will take these songs into many countries... I will provide the finances so that you will be able to do that... These ears are anointed, these eyes are anointed, these feet are anointed to carry my message. Never mind the scars, the wounds... You are in a war... There will be wounds. I will make your head as an adamant.

Chapter 9

Rachael was born in the spring. Jerry and Maggie, our eldest son and his wife, dedicated her to the LORD in the fall of 1977 at the First Baptist Church with Reverend John Lavender ministering. Some time later they began attending Calvary Bible Church. He told me that they had dedicated their other children, Madeline and Tim, there. Jerry was baptized there about 1983 with Reverend Jack Peacock ministering.

October 8, 1980, I was visiting mother and my cousin Yvonell was there. As we were discussing the things of the LORD she prophesied Isaiah 59:19b, "...When the enemy shall come in like a flood, the SPIRIT of the LORD shall lift up a standard against him."

In about 1982 I went to meet Reverend Duane Meadors at the New Life In Christ Church building site. The exterior of the building was completed. The interior was not yet completed and the parking lot was ready to be paved. I was there to figure cost so the company could bid the job. While there the pastor showed me the interior of the building. They had sat a lectern on the unfinished platform. I walked to the lectern and said something like now listen to this to the empty room. Reverend Meadors invited me to visit Amy B. Seibert School where they were holding services. One Sunday morning I did just that. Before I left he asked me to come back that evening and preach. I told him I did not have anything prepared. He told me the LORD will give you something. During the afternoon, I was planning to preach on multiplying the church rather than adding to the church. After about two hours of work on my plan with nothing coming together, the Lord showed me that he wanted to comfort his people and gave me Isaiah 40:1 and comfort verses throughout the rest of Isaiah. That preparation was done in about an hour. I took Rachael, our eldest granddaughter, with me to that service. She was then about five years old. When we arrived home she told grandma, "Grandpa was the pastor." Rev. Meadors invited me back to minister in the new building. I remember a couple of times I sang and played the guitar.

In those days I visited several churches and ministered in music and occasionally in the pulpit. It was the pulpit in a Weedpatch Pentecostal Church. In music at the Faith Lighthouse in Bakersfield and some times in music and once in the pulpit at Fellowship For Christ in Bakersfield. In the Fellowship For Christ, there was an occasion where a lady prophesied, "Your ministry will take you far. You will have a large motor home, it will be brown and white." A few years later we bought an old class A motor home, not large by my standards (only 26 feet), but it was brown and white.

1981 The company was low bidder on a project in Mammoth Lakes and one in June Lake. Willie and I were staying at the Ski and Racket Club. We were able to do that because of the summer rates. I was working the job in June Lake and had weekends off. One Sunday I went to church in Mammoth Lakes where they talked about the HOLY SPIRIT but I saw no evidence of them actually knowing HIM. I began to attend The Church On The Mountain in the community of Lake Crowley. It was obvious that they knew HIM. One Sunday there was prayer for a young lady (with a nice hairdo). Several people approached her from the front and laid hands on her shoulders. I approached her from the back and held my right hand about six inches above her head. I didn't want to mess up that hairdo. After the prayers were finished, she turned around and asked "Who put their hand on my head?" At that moment the HOLY SPIRIT came upon me and my knees became weak, I staggered back and collapsed into a folding chair in the front row. No visible person there had touched her head. She had felt the HAND OF GOD. PRAISE HIS HOLY NAME.

One morning before Willie woke, I was reading Joshua 5:14, "And HE said, Nay; but *as* captain of the host of the LORD am I now come," when an earthquake (6.1 or 6.7 by various reports) hit. Willie woke and started for the rear door. The rear door opened onto a balcony one-half story above the hillside. From the front parking side we were on the third floor. I did not want Willie to be hit by balconies above falling on her so I grabbed her and we stayed in the doorway between the bedroom and the kitchen. There was no apparent damage, we got ready and went to work.

October 23, 1982, 2:05 a.m. I woke from a dream about my brother Bill in the middle of a large number of snakes. The next day, research found the following: Psalm 91:13, "Thou shall tread upon the lion and adder: the young lion and the dragon shalt thou trample under feet," Mark 16:18, "They shall take up serpents; and if they drink any deadly thing, it shall not hurt them, they shall lay hands on the sick and they shall recover." And Luke 10:19, "Behold, I give unto you power to tread on serpents and scorpions, and over all the power of the enemy: and nothing shall by any means hurt you."

November 14, 1982, At the Oildale Assembly Of GOD Church there was a prophesy from the pulpit which was essentially: "I am in your midst by MY SPIRIT to call you unto holiness. Let fire be kindled by MY SPIRIT to behold ... MY SPIRIT searches to turn your heart to me in full and complete surrender. Receive of grace, receive of love, receive of yearning. You will know HIM as the LORD."

Curtis and Sherri Blackwell began attending Oildale Assembly Of GOD. They were a precious young couple that would worship side by side oblivious to anything around them. I was envious of that relationship. My desire was for Willie and I to worship the way they were. While the law tells us not to covet, it is referring to things such as wealth and servants. First Corinthians 12:31 tells us to "Covet the best gifts." The gifts and calling of GOD are without repentance.

During one period of unemployment I was visiting at Spirit Life Center and Reverend Norman Ambrose invited me to preach at the Wednesday Night Service. After the sermon, Reverend Ambrose took up a love offering. I told him I did not come for money. He then said, "If that was what you came for you would not have gotten it." There were only three or four families there that evening. The offering was sixty dollars and really came in handy. GOD still supplies all our needs. Praise HIS NAME. Later I was attending the same church which had moved next door and had a different pastor, Wayne Gibson. In one service, sister Wanda Jones gave an exhortation to change our ways and repent. She was looking out into the congregation at no one in particular and no where near me but I knew the LORD was speaking directly to me.

December 14, 1981, in my daily Bible reading, I underlined most of Isaiah 59: 21, "My SPIRIT that is upon thee, and MY words which I have put in thy mouth, shall not depart out of thy mouth, nor the mouth of thy seed, nor out of the mouth of thy seed's seed, saith the LORD, from henceforth and forever." Then on December 19, 1981, Jerry Leonard quoted the same to me. And on December 29, 1981, Juanita Essert also quoted it to me.

September 26, 1983, While visiting Jerry Leonard in Taft he shared Job 33:25, "His flesh shall be fresher than a child's: He shall return to the days of his youth." Also he had a strong tingling and a burning in his ear and said, "The LORD is going to speak in your ear more clearly than ever before."

January 26, 1984, I was in Taft and very thirsty. I stopped at Jerry Leonard's barber shop. He quoted a portion of Revelation 21:6 to me. "I AM ALPHA and OMEGA, the beginning and the end. I Will give unto him that is athirst of the fountain of the water of life freely." On an earlier visit to see Mr. Leonard he had shared Job 33:14-16, "For GOD speaketh once, yea twice, *yet man* perceiveth it not. In a dream, in a vision of the night, when deep sleep falleth upon men, in slumberings upon the bed; Then HE openeth the ears of men, and sealeth their instruction."

Jerry Leonard, president of the Taft Chapter of FGBMFI, invited me to minister in music one Saturday at a breakfast meeting. David Joiner, Senior Pastor at Liberty Christian Center, ministered the word. Ray and Virginia Cook also came to support my ministry.

In the late 1980s I was attending churches which only met Sunday mornings. I would visit other churches for the evening services. On one of those visits I had a single word for the man playing the organ and told the pastor about it but he told me to give the man the word myself. It did not make any sense to me but I told the musician the word and he said that was the answer he was seeking from the LORD regarding the direction his ministry was to take.

There were, over the months, several visits to that church. At one time there was a musical group from Texas and a message in tongues was given them. The LORD gave me the interpretation. It was essentially As you drive down the roads you do not see what is over the hill or around the corner, even so it is with your walk with me. You know the road is there and you know that I AM there.

On another visit I had a message in tongues and started giving it. The pastor stopped me and said "That is not the SPIRIT OF JESUS." I try to always be in obedience to those in authority so I sat quietly until the service ended. I went outside and a young man was there who had been inside when I was stopped. He asked me what was that which happened in there? Told him I did not know, then the SPIRIT moved and stomped my feet on the sidewalk. I never went back. About six months later that pastor was at a FGBMFI dinner meeting and stopped me and told me the LORD had told him that he should not have done that. He told me we should have waited on the LORD. He then told me that he had heard me give interpretations almost word for word for what the LORD was giving him. Thank YOU, LORD, for that confirmation.

An April 9, 1989, A message recorded by a lady in the church and a typed copy handed to me later, said, message given by Ed Coble & interpretation given by Bob Horttor. "I am in your presence by MY SPIRIT. Worship ME in the beauty of holiness. Worship me in truth and spirit for I have loved you with an everlasting love. I have chosen you to be MY servants and do MY bidding and walk in MY footprints, and I will bless you and I will prosper you and honor you as you honor ME." The lady's record had another message without identifying the prophet. It said, "I have loved you with an everlasting love. I am touched by the feelings of your infirmities,, EVERY ANSWER TO EVERY PROBLEM IN YOUR LIFE RESTS IN ME!"

Perhaps 1988 or 1989, I began to tell GOD that I was to tired to look for scriptures in the night when HE would awaken me for that purpose according to the signs that **I had chosen.** Therefore there was a period of time when the LORD did not wake me for that purpose. Sometime in the spring or summer of 1990, HE again began to wake me at exactly on the hour or on the half hour. For a few months I did not record what HE was telling me. Then on October 28, 1990, at 4:30 a.m. I woke and pulled a card from the file which read: "As the FATHER has sent ME, even so send I you."

In the morning BIBLE reading of November 2, 1990, at 5:25 a.m. from the New American Standard was Psalm 102:18-21, "This will be written for the generation to come; THAT A PEOPLE YET TO BE CREATED MAY PRAISE THE LORD. For HE looked down from his holy height; from heaven the LORD gazed upon the earth, to hear the groaning of the prisoner, to set FREE THOSE THAT WERE DOOMED TO DEATH; THAT MEN MAY TELL OF THE NAME OF THE LORD in Zion, and his praise in Jerusalem."

November 6, 1990, NAS, Proverbs 3:1 "... do not forget MY teaching, But let your heart keep MY commandments; for length of days and years of life and peace they will add to you." And the next day Proverbs 22:19b-21a, "I have taught you today, even you. Have not I written to you excellent things of counsels and Knowledge, to make you know the certainty of the WORDS OF TRUTH." Then at midnight of the 12th from the card file Isaiah 50:7 "FOR the LORD GOD will help me; therefore shall I not be confounded... I know that I shall not be put to shame." November 14, 1990, NAS, Isaiah 41:9b, "You are my servant. I have chosen you and not rejected you." Also Isaiah 42:6a, '**I am the LORD, I have called you in righteousness,** I will also hold you by the hand and watch over you."

November 19. 1990, 1:00am from card file. Ephesians 6:11 "Put on the whole armor of GOD, that ye may be able to stand against the wiles of the devil. And Hebrews 4:14, "Inasmuch as we have a great HIGH PRIEST....JESUS the son of GOD, let us never stop trusting HIM." November 19, 1990, I woke from a dream at 3:59am. In that dream a large blond man with a neck brace was being healed as I was **loudly commanding him to be healed in JESUS' NAME**.

December 6, 1990, As I was preparing my breakfast, I began to think about Willie's arthritis and how it is beginning to affect her hands. I began to think that I should just place a hand on her and say "Be healed in JESUS NAME" once a day until she is healed. Since her brother had spent the night and they had continued their visit well after I had gone to bed, I had only checked to see if she wanted to sleep in. She said, "yes," then said, she had been dreaming that her hands were straightening out. On the way home from work, I was rejoicing because the LORD was confirming to Willie what was in my heart. When I asked her about her dream, she had forgotten it and insisted that she **did not** have a dream and accused me of "going crazy." April 18, 1991, 3:00 a.m. from my pocket BIBLE, Luke 18:2-8, parable about the unjust judge and the widow that kept coming until he avenged her. I associated that with the need for me to keep on praying for Willie to be healed.

Chapter 10

March 22, 1991, Eddie was spending the night with us and he told me he wants a "HOLY BIBLE" either for Christmas or his birthday (only a few days apart). At that time I got out the New Testament the church had given us for him when Grandma Willie and I had dedicated him to the LORD. I asked him if he wants a black, brown or blue BIBLE. He said if you can't get a blue one I'll take a black one. Praise GOD. He asked me if Melissa has a BIBLE and if she has ever been dedicated. I don't know about the BIBLE but she has not been dedicated (in a formal ceremony) to the LORD. I told him at her age she can be "saved" and is probably to old to be dedicated. Note to myself, "Maybe not." Another note, "I have long ago dedicated her to the LORD in my private times with HIM." I love you LORD. Only days later there was the episode around the TV with Melissa and grandpa watching Rev Schambach which was recorded in chapter 6.

Night of April 16, 1991, Sometime during the night, I dreamed that I was building buildings with a silty material which kept on falling off the buildings. I don't know if the buildings were real or only sand castles. As I write this GOD is saying HE is the glue that holds things together.

September 8, 1991, Evening service at Faith Tabernacle on North Kern Street, Pastor Tim Goolsby prophesied something like "Bob, you must begin to minister, you must be a soft vessel, yielded to the LORD. In that same service another man prophesied We must preach, we must do the things that GOD would have us to do. God is not through with you yet."

Saturday November 16, 1991, I was grade checking finish grading for aggregate base on the airport job at Shafter when the superintendent, Bob Stevens, came on the job. He asked me if we were finished with that work. I told him we need to make one more pass. He asked if we had made a pass with the laser controlling the blade. I assured him that we had. Without giving me a chance to explain that we needed a pass with the sonar to match the joint, he ordered us to put the equipment away and stop for the day. The following Monday, after work started, the inspector rejected the work which had an asphalt seal placed on top of it. One pass of the blade before the seal was placed would have saved the work. Mr. Stevens was angry, and after several minutes of his complaints, I told him, "If you don't like my work, that's easy to fix." He fired me.

November 22, 1991, Still out of work and temporarily out of supplies for finishing the closet I was building in the patio room, I began to read a used book I had bought, "LISTEN FOR THE WHISPERS" by Esther Kerr Rusthoi. At 2:50 p.m. I was reading in chapter 2, titled SONGS OF DELIVERANCE. Near the end of the chapter was this prophesy, "There is yet another song of deliverance **which shall be sung**, and they sang a new song, saying Thou art worthy...for thou wast slain, and hast redeemed us to GOD by thy blood... and hast made us unto our GOD kings and priests: and we shall reign on the earth. And I beheld, and I heard the voice of many angels round about the throne and the beasts and elders: and the number of them was ten thousand times ten thousand and thousands of thousands; Saying with a loud voice, Worthy is the LAMB that was slain to receive power, and riches, and wisdom, and strength, and honor, and glory, and blessing. And every creature which is in heaven and on the earth...heard I saying...<u>blessing and honor and glory and power</u>..be unto him that sitteth upon the throne, and unto the LAMB forever and ever!" This seemed to me to be a reference to a song I had written fourteen years before I had read anything in that book. The book had been copyrighted twenty five years before I had written the song. In chapter 4 of this book I had the thought, "ten thousand times ten thousand." Then in chapter 5, I wrote the song I gave the title ONE HUNDRED MILLION.

February 22, 1992, Richard Goldberg called around 7:00 or 7:30 Near the end of our visit he said "I have a word." The message was to long for me to remember all of it but it included such phrases as: You are a part of my work, That desire in your heart, I put there while you were in the womb. The anointing will drip from your hands and your fingers, ... around the world... many will come... You will be part of the work, I will not leave you out.

July 9, 1992, Around 9:30 or 10:00 p.m. Willie told me "I have had a strange dream" and said that she could not remember what it was but said that it meant something. The next day I prayed that the LORD would show me the dream and the interpretation and to let Willie know that HE (THE LORD) was the revealer of dreams. That night I dreamed of black spots or shapes, without corners, moving, changing shapes, getting smaller then disappearing. This was on a blue background. My thoughts were that the black shapes were demons, writhing, getting weaker then being gone. PRAISE GOD!!!

August 31, 1992, Because of a tightness in my chest I underwent a heart Catherization to check for blocked arteries. The test showed no blockage but I was advised that I had a left branch bundle block. On September 2nd Dr. Ishimori advised me to not get hot or work hard enough to sweat because that causes blood clots. In late October or early November 1992, the first strong rain of the season came. Willie was very angry because the patio roof was leaking. The more it rained, the harder the work became to protect the "stuff" in the patio room. As the rain increased, the work increased and the sweat began pouring, I began to think that Willie was more concerned about the things that I had provided than about me. It was only after I had wallowed in this self pity for several minutes when the LORD revealed that this is the way we treat HIM. We are guilty of seeking his provisions rather than seeking HIM. Help us LORD.

In a dream, I was driving a pickup and looked at the windshield which had about a dozen drops of water the size of my little finger nail. Then I leaned forward and looked at the sky. It had black clouds everywhere with no clear place at all. Then THE LORD revealed this, "The drops you see on the windshield are what you have seen the HOLY GHOST do until now. The storm you see is what HE is about to do."

October 26, 1992, I fell short and missed the mark several times during the day and the evening. The next morning I woke at 5:30 a.m. and pulled from the card file Hebrews 4:16, "Let us approach the throne of grace with confidence, that we may receive mercy for our failures and grace for well-timed help." This was very meaningful because of my failures. Thank you LORD. November 17, 1992, 4:30 a.m. from the card file, I John 2:1, "If any man sin, we have an advocate with the FATHER, JESUS CHRIST the righteous."

December 11, 1993, around 6:30 p.m. Margaret Kapchinski called to say she missed me at church. Before she finished visiting she said, "GOD is going to open a door <u>wide</u> for you to tell others how you feel about HIM."

March 1, 1994, 6:00 a.m. I awoke from this dream. I saw a large hot grill with a map of Africa on it's surface. The national boundaries were somewhat different than what I recalled. As I watched, blue flames began to come up from a few countries then quickly spread to the entire continent except for one country which I took to be inland perhaps made up of parts of Congo and Zaire and possibly including a portion of Central African Republic.

May 1, 1994 evening service Pastor Wayne Gibson called forth the song leader and the musicians (I was one of the guitar players) and anointed each one for service to the LORD and his prayer was for a double portion for each one.

Dad went into eternity on June 3, 1994. I preached his funeral. Part of the message was I Thessalonians 4: 13-17, "But I would not have you to be ignorant, brethren, concerning them which are asleep....we which are alive and remain....shall not prevent them which are asleep. ....the dead in CHRIST shall rise first: Then we which are alive and remain shall be caught up with them in the clouds, to meet the LORD in the air....comfort one another with these words."

On the evening of October 27, 1994, while talking to Adam; Terry's son, our grandson; about the LORD, I told him to be saved you must believe that GOD raised JESUS from the dead and confess HIM with your mouth when Jacquie, Terry's daughter, said, "I've done that."

February 14, 1995, 3:00 a.m. I woke from dreaming, I was at a very large meeting with people in three or four rooms. I was laying hands on some individuals who were immediately "slain in the SPIRIT." Later I was seated in a chair looking at some cards and began to weep. A large group of men gathered around me and I fell over backwards in the chair although completely surrounded by those men. After I woke I began to pray for my pastor because the LORD brought him to mind.

August 3, 1995, in the early evening Terry and Adam came over to our house. Adam wanted me to to pray to get "the devil" out of him. Rather than do that I used an old VOICE magazine and went through their "Six Steps To Salvation" with him, then led him in the sinners prayer written in it. After that Adam's grandma, Willie, said to Adam "Some day you'll have to do that with me." So I told Adam to do it now. He read the sinners prayer for grandma to pray after him, which she did. Isn't GOD good.

Chapter 11

Sunday morning October 1, 1995, I woke from dreaming . I was with a group of people on the sidewalk outside a building during a break or an intermission from the activities inside the building. I was facing a person as he said "Glory." Immediately the SPIRIT moved me to yell "GLORY" and then do a dance on the sidewalk and the lawn as everyone around was watching.

October 22, 1995, in the early afternoon around 1:30 or 2:30 I began having some sharp pains in the right side of my heart. I felt like just lying down but I had told Terry that his mom and I would get the pickup to haul some vertical blinds that we were planning to buy for the condo. While we were out shopping , taking the blinds to the condo, buying gas and until about the time for church, the pains hit about every half hour so I thought about staying home. However, I went to New Creation Harvest Center and at about 6:30 when they were taking prayer requests, I shared with them about the pains and asked for prayer. Then I told the congregation and Reverend Marty Manning, who was taking prayer requests, that I was being obedient to what the LORD had told us to do in the fifth chapter of James, which is to call for the elders of the church and let them anoint him with oil and the prayer of faith will heal the sick and if he has committed any sin, it shall be forgiven him. Reverend Manning then called me forward and called men around me to anoint me and pray. Then he resumed taking prayer requests.

September 13, 1996, I woke from dreaming a man was prophesying over me saying, "Why aren't you teaching the children music?" In a dream the following night two people had me strapped to a gurney. They had a band with several small needles made into the band and were were sticking the needles into my forehead, I cried out, "I don't want any tattoos on my head." They said, "We are only giving you an anesthetic in case he has to operate."

October 26, 1997, Sunday evening at GOD's Cornerstone Church (New name and new location of the New Creation Harvest Center) the senior pastor, Jerry Harvey, was absent and the associate pastor, Marty Manning, was preparing to anoint Dan's wife, Rosa, some time after he had called me forward to help pray for some needs of the congregation. Rosa and three other ladies were going to pray in the ladies bathroom about a cold feeling that had been felt in there. Before Pastor Manning had anointed Rosa, she was holding her hands up about shoulder high, with the palms facing us when both I and the pastor noticed oil covering the tips of all her fingers and thumbs. On her right hand it was past the distal joint on all digits and was about to that joint on her left hand.

I visited where Jerry Harvey was pastoring, Hope Tabernacle. The congregation had moved and had a new name for the church. As I was leaving the building after the service was over, I overheard the Associate Pastor, Pete Bond, telling Rev. Harvey that he (Rev. Bond) would take care of it. I walked out into the back lot parking area got into my car and started driving out of the lot. As I was leaving the parking lot Rev. Bond stopped me and asked me to bring the message for Wednesday Night. I took his number and said I would get back to him after I had talked to my wife. Willie agreed to allow me out of the house for that purpose. I took my mandolin, sang a special, and delivered a message from the pulpit.

Saturday morning February 14, 1998, I woke from dreaming I had been visiting a congregation where they were praying with various ones. A certain young man tried several times to get one of those to pray for him to have a healing. When all ignored him, I stood up and said, "I'll pray for you." I came near and reached over another person and touched the young man, who immediately fell backwards to the floor. Only a short prayer was prayed and when there was confusion on the faces of a few, I said to one, "This can be found in the 12th chapter of 1st Corinthians." I then began to look for my BIBLE but could not find it. There were many birthday and valentine cards on the floor. I awoke....

Summer 1999   Eddie had finished his junior year at Spring Creek High School. His dad and Carol were planning a vacation and had determined that he could not stay by himself. Eddie had found a summer job and did not want to lose it. So we went early enough to be there before they left and planned to stay long enough to visit with them after their return. I contacted Christian Life Fellowship and learned they were meeting at Spring Creek Middle School. The pastors were Ron and Vicky Perkins. Rod and Chris Wilson were music ministers. That was my home church for about six weeks. They were meeting in the gym and had to set up chairs on the floor of the basketball court. They spread quilts on the floor where they would be praying. Nearly all of the ones prayed for fell into the hands of catchers who let them down to the floor on the quilts. In one meeting there were several people lined up side by side for prayer. Chris Wilson joined Pastor Perkins praying for each of those in the line. Chris was giving each one of them a personal prophesy. I was hungry to hear from GOD so went to the end of the line and waited for them to arrive. When they got to me I touched Chris on the forehead and she collapsed in a pile where she had been standing. I guess I did not need a prophesy. GOD knows how to work around us. Praise HIS HOLY NAME.

It was at this time I was taking a heart medicine that was making it difficult for me to walk. After talking to the doctor I discontinued its use. To go into the back yard, I would walk out the front door because there was one less step to the ground. I began going to an aquatic exercise program. It was there that I met Reverend Charles Woodworth of Saint Andrew's United Methodist Church. As we became acquainted, he invited me to sing a special at his church. He asked me to sing This Old House. He gave me a copy of the music and lyrics. In those days St. Andrew's was meeting twice a month and Rev. Woodworth and his wife were attending Trinity United Methodist Church on alternate Sundays. He invited me to sing a special there August 6, 2000. I sang one of my own songs there. He was gracious enough to invite me back to St. Andrew's for another special on September 17, 2000. I believe I sang two of my own songs at that time.

There were weekends when Willie wanted to visit her sister, Betty, and her niece, Annette, in Visalia. When we were there I would visit The Assembly Of GOD just north of the circle. Reverend Arvil Kilgore was the pastor. One evening Larry and Ann Diamond, Missionaries to Ireland, were ministering. The LORD gave me a word for them. On a later weekend Betty said she needed prayer for her hip. I had prayed a few weeks earlier for her leg and that was not bothering her anymore. She then shared that the problem had included her hip but did not request prayer for that. I asked Annette to place her hand on her mother at the affected place. I then placed a hand on Annette's shoulder and prayed in the Spirit and with understanding. After the prayer was over Betty said it was hot where Annette's hand had been and Annette said it was hot where my hand had been. The hip had been healed. Thank YOU LORD.

Reverend Ardath and Lulu Faye Dawson had rented one room in the Rassmussen Senior Center for two hours every Sunday for Agape Love Church facilities. I knew some of the members and visited there. Reverend Dawson liked to let the HOLY GHOST have HIS freedom so I made that my church home. His routine was about an hour of worship and then almost an hour of sermon followed by prayer. I took my guitar and played with the musicians in the worship services. Reverend Dawson began to treat me like an associate pastor. There were times he asked me to bring the message to the people. One Sunday he had asked me to preach the next Sunday. I worked all week on a sermon and when I arrived at church, I told him I only had about five minutes. He went through the worship part of the service and turned it over to me. That five minutes turned into a full length sermon. After the services were over a sister, they all called Aunt Mary, shared with us that she had seen an angel who was the height of the door standing behind me near the door.

Another Sunday I was ministering on the Baptism of the HOLY GHOST. All through the sermon I had the feeling this was not necessary because I thought everyone there had been baptized by JESUS. After the sermon was over I gave an altar call and a daughter of one of the ladies came forward and received the baptism. This just goes to show that when GOD tells you to do something do it even when the enemy tries to tell you it is pointless. GOD really knows what each of us need.

I asked Reverend Dawson if we could have my friend Richard Goldberg share with us some Sunday morning. I invited Richard and he graciously consented. The day he was there he shared about the time he was ministering with a team aboard a ship. Richard said he had hoped to see the whales so he prayed and asked God to let him see the whales. The next morning whales were swimming around the ship. Richard said he then went into the water and swam with the whales. GOD is so good.

I emailed Richard the above paragraph and this:
I am pretty sure this is not exactly the way it should be. I think you were much closer than just swimming.

Your help and blessings would be greatly appreciated.

Wednesday evening May 24, 1989, the LORD gave you three visions which you shared with me. The note I made was as follows:
    1 GOD
        I will not fail thee or forsake thee.
        I Samuel 17:47 The battle is the LORD's.
    2 The body
        I Corinthians 12:12 ....one body.
    3 The harvest
My memory of the other details has grown dim.
His response included this.

> Greetings Bob!
>
> Yes I often share the story of the whale. The most amazing thing about it to me is that it wasn't necessarily a prayer to help anyone or anything just a boyish desire of my heart. To me it was God saying I love you Richard with the simplest of acts, granting my request. No one was saved or healed but it let me know that God the Father, the architect and administrator of the universe heard my prayer and answered it. When the other guys on the ship saw the whale they said "Richard your whale is here."
>
> Yes three visions;
>
> wow, such an important thing in my heart.

We must see and understand that God is with us and he fights for us.

The body - this is perhaps the area that we struggle with the most. Each person has THEIR own part to fulfill. I am always amazed when I hear on a sports report that some big strong multimillion dollar paid athlete is unable to do his job because of something called "turf toe". Are you telling me this sports machine of a body cannot function because his toe hurts? Even a toe in the body of Christ is important.

Some speak, some pray, some preach, some serve a glass of cold water in his name, they ALL make a difference. The ministry of the body to the body is how we stay healthy, grow and learn many things.

The harvest - It is impossible to understand the heart of God without understanding the lost and his desire save them and walk with them. There is something about not being too focused on our own lives and situation, having the lost in front of us and on our hearts puts us in God the Father's frame of mind.

This is kind of a silly thought but it's like asking to see someone's most valuable possession, the most they ever paid for anything. In God's case the most he ever paid was for the lost. He gave his Son for them and desperately wants to gather them all to Himself to save them and to walk and talk with them in the cool of the day.

Hope that helps..

Richard

February 8, 1998, after I had preached at Agape Love Church, during the prayer time, Sister Wanda Jones was saying to me that the water was past the ankles and to the knees like in the book of Isaiah. I told her that the waters that flowed out from the throne in the book of Revelation brought healing wherever they went. Lula Faye Dawson then said to me that I will lay hands on people and "they will be healed."

Chapter 12

Early in the year of 2003 I started becoming exhausted after only a few minutes of exercise and shared that with Dr. Ishimori, my cardiologist. He decided that it was time to implant a pacemaker. He referred me to Dr. Nalos, who chose the Medtronic model 7272 with a defibrillator. Early on I had trouble with the lead to the left ventricle. After about a year Dr. Nalos went in to place a new lead. You are not completely out when they do those procedures. Just as the new lead was in place and the doctor was removing the implant tool the lead became dislodged and he had to place it again. When it was in place the second time, Dr. Nalos said "Someone must have been praying." A male voice said, "I have been." Dr. Nalos said "I was, too." Then I said, "That makes it unanimous."

July 2003 I underwent a procedure to replace my left knee. I don't remember the four days in the Surgical Hospital. They said I had required four units of blood. I do remember the ambulance ride to the rehab hospital. The hospital staff put my leg on a machine to flex the joint. The machine kept pinching my seat and in my effort to remove it I kicked the machine with my other foot. I also accidentally kicked Willie while she was trying to help me. I was there eight days before being released. I shared a two bed room with three different men (one at a time). The second man was only there a couple of days but while he was there his pastor came to share communion with him and asked if I wanted to join them. We broke the bread and drank the wine. I was surprised that it was actually wine. Thank you for sharing communion, Pastor.

Early in 2004 my right knee collapsed as I walked between the car and the fence. I grabbed the top of the fence to avoid a fall. Willie saw me from the house and said we are going to get that knee fixed. I made an appointment for April 1, 2004 (Is April Fool's Day a good time for surgery?). Because of my demeanor after the first knee surgery, Willie packed a suitcase to visit her sister until I was to be released from the rehab hospital. The night before the surgery I spent asking the LORD to make me HIS representative rather than what I had done before. We arrived at the hospital before 7:30 at 10:30 I went into the operating room. I was wide awake at 2:30 when Willie entered the recovery room. Already sitting up in bed, I said, "Hello, Beautiful." Willie decided to cancel her trip. That afternoon I used the walker to go about 180 feet. Still later that day it was used to help me go about 300 feet. It was not necessary to go to the rehab hospital. Thank GOD for HIS moving on and for us.

In the fall of 2006 I shared with my pastor, Reverend David Albright, how he had been a blessing to me back in the 1970s or 1980s when he was preaching on the radio. In his sermons he would say "and you, Sir" and GOD would use that to speak directly to me as if GOD had put HIS finger to my chest and said "and you, Sir." After sharing that with the pastor I shared that with Sister Lois Miller who then told me that I should write a song about that. The song written was called YOU SIR.

Pastor Albright's first sermon in 2007 was about GOD having us where he wants us for a reason. I wrote a song Which I called WHO KNOWS. I had written three verses and was getting ready to register a copyright when I felt that my president was being unreasonably accused for doing what GOD had told him to do. I could not leave the song without adding a verse about presidents. Abe had heard the LORD say "divided, you'll not stand," and Harry knew the LORD was color blind and integrated the military services.

A few weeks later Rex Leith came to me after the service and told me the LORD had given him this phrase, "From the cross to the crown" He asked his wife, Lila, what he should do with it. She told him, "Give it to Bob." I wrote a song from that word. The name is FROM THE CROSS TO THE CROWN.

In the fall of 2006 four dreams came to me. The first one was of a young lady in a portrait view. The next one was the same lady and a stemmed glass filled with crystal clear water. In the third dream there was a ball of fire with a man and a woman silhouetted only about five percent of the height of the ball. The fourth was me very near an artesian well with crystal clear water in a gigantic spray much higher than my head.

January 23, 2007, early morning I awoke from a worldly dream and was very grieved because of that dream. A short time later, awake or asleep? I don't know, I saw a filthy sheet like the one John had worn and lost when he fled from the mob that arrested JESUS. The sheet was out in space with me just behind and to its left looking at the earth. The filthy sheet began moving towards the earth, flew up over and around the earth and into a large open door on a furnace. The furnace then became the sun. This is an example of how the FATHER takes our sins and removes them farther than the East is from the West.

As I entered the Ninety Nine Cent Store, a young man who had tattoos around his neck, up the side of his face, and half way across his forehead saw my JESUS SAVES belt buckle and engaged me in fellowship. After we had visited for a few minutes we went separate ways. A few minutes later he sought me out and asked for prayer for a sore foot. I knelt to place my right hand on his foot and prayed in the SPIRIT there inside the front of the store. GOD has admonished us to be "instant in season, out of season."

January 8, 2008, early morning, I woke from dreaming I saw a cardboard box about eighteen by eighteen by six inches high, opened with a gift box (the size of an earring box or a ring box) inside the larger box. On the floor were about three of the smaller sized gift boxes. These gifts are precious to the world but the gifts from GOD are eternal and very precious indeed.

January 5, 2008, I went to Food Maxx for a few items and because of the store's arrangement, it was necessary to go through the produce section. I saw Margaret Rector there inspecting some items. I pushed my cart in front of hers and kidding her I said, "If I didn't love the LORD, I wouldn't talk to you." There was recognition, a smile then a hug and she started prophesying .."The time is short...your time is short...you will be in the rapture, it is coming soon."

Christmas Day 2008, My cousin, Yvonell Wegener, called. It was a very nice surprise. I did not know where she had gone or how to locate her. After we had caught up, I asked if she had a word for me. As she thought on it she said, "There is a change around you. There is a deep stirring around you. Reaching deep like a cake stirring. Like a leaf in a book turning over and you are going to read what's written. Others will not be able to read it. It may be ...like in Hebrew. You will be dancing around like a spinning." She then said, "Look at Psalm 25:14." In the King James version it reads: "The secret of the LORD is with them that fear HIM; and HE will shew them HIS covenant."

In a recent sermon Pastor Albright held up his Bible and mentioned Sixty Six Books. I started working on a new song and will use that for the title.

January 15, 1983, I underlined Isaiah 38:20 in the Nelson Large Print, King James version "The LORD was ready to save me: therefore we will sing my songs to the stringed instruments all the days of our life in the house of the LORD."

Chapter 13

January 4, 1982: Hosea 10:12, "Sow to yourself in righteousness, reap in mercy, break up your fallow ground: for it is time to seek the LORD, till HE come and rain righteousness upon you."

January 4, 1983, Psalm 69:30-32, "I will praise the name of GOD with a song, and will magnify HIM with thanksgiving, *This* also shall please the LORD better than an ox *or* bullock that hath horns and hoofs, The humble shall see *this, and* be glad: and your heart shall live that seek GOD."

Proverbs 10: 22, "The blessing of the LORD, it maketh rich, and HE addeth no sorrow with it."

July 17, 1981: Jeremiah 1: 5 & 7, "Before I formed thee in the belly, I knew thee; and before thou camest out of the womb I sanctified thee, *and* I ordained thee a prophet unto the nations....Say not, I am a child: for thou shalt go to all that I send thee, and whatsoever I command thee thou shalt speak."

December 22, 1981 and May 30, 1983 Jeremiah 45:5b, "..but thy life will I give thee for a prey in all places whither thou goest."

May 5, 1985 In Sunday School Class Micah 6:8, "HE hath shewed thee, O man, what is good; and what doth the LORD require of thee, but to do justly, and to love mercy, and to walk humbly with thy GOD?"

January 15, 1982: Luke 4:18, "The SPIRIT OF THE LORD is upon me, because HE hath anointed me to preach the gospel to the poor; HE hath sent me to heal the brokenhearted, to preach deliverance to the captives, and recovering of sight to the blind, to set at liberty them that are bruised," Then June 17, 1984 Luke 4:19, "To preach the acceptable year of the LORD."

Acts 2:21&39, "...whosoever shall call on the name of the LORD shall be saved. ....For the promise is unto you, and to your children, and to all that are afar off, *even* as many as the LORD our GOD shall call."

Romans 10:9&10, "That if thou shalt confess with thy mouth the LORD JESUS, and shalt believe in thine heart that GOD hath raised HIM from the dead, thou shalt be saved. For with the heart man believeth unto righteousness; and with the mouth confession is made unto salvation." Verse 14b, "...how shall they hear without a preacher?" And 11:29, "For the gifts and calling of GOD are without repentance."

February 5, 1982, I Peter 5:2&3, "Feed the flock of GOD which is among you, taking the oversight *thereof*, not by constraint, but willingly; nor for filthy lucre, but of a ready mind; Neither as being lords over GOD's heritage, but being ensamples to the flock." And verse 5b, "...Yea, all *of you* be subject one to another, and be clothed with humility...."

February 28, 1983, II Peter 1:10&11, "Wherefore the rather, brethren, give diligence to make your calling and election sure; for if ye do these things, ye shall never fall; For so an entrance shall be ministered unto you abundantly into the everlasting kingdom of our LORD and SAVOUR JESUS CHRIST."

The LORD will speak to you: in an audible voice, in a vision, in a dream, in HIS WORD, through tongues and interpretation, through prophesy, a song, or even from the pages of a book written by an author anointed by GOD HIMSELF. Some time you will be lead through trials and tribulations, and never know that it was in order for you to be equipped for service or to avoid a much worse situation which GOD only knew would be happening where you had intended to go.

John 14:12-15, "Verily, verily, I say unto you, He that believeth on ME, the works that I do shall he do also; and greater *works* than these shall he do; *because* I go unto MY FATHER. And whatsoever ye shall ask in MY NAME, that will I do, that the FATHER may be glorified in the SON. If ye shall ask any thing in MY NAME. I will do *it*." Verse 26, "But the COMFORTER, *which* is the HOLY GHOST, whom the FATHER will send in MY NAME, HE shall teach you all things, and bring all things to your remembrance, whatsoever I have said unto you.' 15:16, "Ye have not chosen ME, but I have chosen you, and ordained you, that ye should go and bring forth fruit, and *that* your fruit should remain; that whatsoever ye shall ask of the FATHER in MY NAME, HE may give it you." 16:13a, ".When HE, THE SPIRIT OF TRUTH, is come, HE will guide you into all truth..."

JESUS HIMSELF prayed for **you** in John 17:20, "Neither pray I for these alone, but for them also which shall believe on ME through their word."

Do you need joy in your life? Read John 16:24, "Hitherto have ye asked nothing in MY NAME; ask and ye shall receive, that your joy may be full." Revelation 5:8b, "...Golden vials full of odours. which are the prayers of saints." shows us how much our prayers are valued in heaven. I Corinthians 14:31, "For ye may **all** prophesy one by one, that all may learn, and all may be comforted."

I often hear GOD's promises quoted without ever hearing the condition connected to the promise. You cannot claim a promise GOD has made unless you meet the condition. When a condition has been met for a promise it becomes a contract. GOD will never breach HIS contract but we can. If we turn away from the condition we have breached the contract.

If you want to dwell in the land in safety and eat your fill then the conditions are, "Ye shall do my statues, and keep my judgments, and do them." Leviticus 25:18&19.

Deuteronomy Chapter 28 verses one and two give conditions for blessings from there through verse thirteen. Verses sixteen through sixty eight show the curses that will come if we do not obey the conditions.

Want your sins forgiven and your land healed? Be obedient to II Chronicles 7:14, "If MY people, which are called by MY NAME, shall humble themselves, and pray, and seek MY FACE, and turn from their wicked ways, then will I hear from heaven, and will forgive their sin, and will heal their land."

February 4, 1982, 5:54 a.m. Hebrews 12:13, "And make straight paths for your feet, lest that which is lame be turned out of the way; but let it rather be healed."

February 3, 1983, 5:40 a.m. Joel 3:13, "put ye in the sickle, for the harvest is ripe: ..."

Joel 2:17, "Let the priests, the ministers of the LORD, weep between the porch and the altar, and let them say, Spare thy people, O LORD, and give not thine heritage to reproach..."

Chapter 14

A few examples of promises and their conditions are included here for your consideration.

Promise	Condition
Strengthen thine heart.	Psalm 27:14, "Wait on the LORD: be of good courage, ...wait I say on the LORD."
HE shall strengthen your heart.	Psalm 31:24, "Be of good courage, ...all ye that hope in the LORD."
Renew your strength,...run and not be weary, walk and not faint.	Isaiah 40:31, "They that wait upon the LORD shall ....."
See your grandchildren and peace upon Israel	Psalm 128:1 & 6, "Blessed is every one that feareth the LORD; that walketh in HIS ways."
Be at peace with your enemies	Proverbs 16:7, "When a man's ways please the LORD.. HE maketh even his enemies to be at peace with him."
Your thoughts established.	Proverbs 16:3, "Commit thy works unto the LORD, and thy thoughts **shall** be established."
Be my mouth.	Jeremiah 15:19, "... Thus

saith the LORD, If thou return, then I will bring thee again, and thou shall stand before ME; and if thou take forth the precious from the vile, thou shall be as MY mouth..."

Live forever.

Psalm 125:1, "They that trust in the LORD shall be as Mount Zion, which cannot be removed *but* abideth forever."

Enter into the place GOD chose to set HIS NAME.

Nehemiah 1:9, "... turn unto me and keep my commandments, and do them; though there were of you cast out unto the uttermost part of the heaven, yet will I gather them from thence, and will bring them unto the place that I have chosen to set MY name there."

As the family grew Jacquie married Jayson Edington. They had a daughter they named Journey. September 22, 2002, the family gathered at Riverview Assembly Of GOD Church to witness them dedicate Journey to the LORD. The Pastor, Reverend Don Skaggs, ministered in the service.

Ezra told King Artaxerxes "The hand of our GOD is upon **all** them for good that seek HIM; but HIS power and HIS wrath is against **all** them that forsake HIM."

Daniel survived the lion's den because he was faithful. Shadrach, Meshach and Abednego survived the fiery furnace because they refused to worship the idol that King Nebuchadnezzar had ordered to be worshiped. Moses was saved from the river because his parents were GOD fearing people. Noah and his family were saved from the flood because they were willing to work for one hundred years building a ship. They simply believed GOD.

January 28, 1981, Deuteronomy 11:13-17, "And it shall come to pass, if ye shall harken diligently unto my commandments which I command you this day, to love the LORD your GOD, and to serve HIM with all your heart and with all your soul, that I will give you the rain of your land in his due season, the first rain and the latter rain, that thou mayest gather in thy corn, and thy wine, and thine oil. And I will send grass in thy fields for thy cattle, that thou mayest eat and be full. Take heed to yourselves, that your heart be not deceived, and ye turn aside, and serve other gods, and worship them; and then the LORD's wrath be kindled against you, and HE shut up the heaven, that there be no rain, and that the land yield not her fruit; and *lest* ye perish quickly from off the good land which the good LORD giveth you."

II Chronicles 16:9a, "...The eyes of the LORD run to and fro throughout the whole earth, to shew HIMSELF strong in the behalf of *them* whose heart is perfect toward HIM."

July 8, 1984, Sermon both morning and evening Romans 12:2, "And be not conformed to this world: but be ye transformed by the renewing of your mind, that ye may prove what *is* that good, and acceptable, and perfect, will of GOD."

The danger of sinning against the HOLY GHOST by attributing HIS works to the devil is best shown in Matthew 12:31 & 32, "Wherefore I say unto you, All manner of sin shall be forgiven unto men: but the blasphemy *against* the *HOLY* GHOST shall not be forgiven unto men. And whosoever speaketh a word against the SON OF MAN, it shall be forgiven him: but whosoever speaketh against the HOLY GHOST, it shall not be forgiven him, neither in this world, neither in the world to come."

Proverbs 2:10-12, "When wisdom enterth into thine heart, and knowledge is pleasant unto thy soul; Discretion shall preserve thee, understanding shall keep thee: to deliver thee from the way of the evil man, from the man that speaketh froward things..." Proverbs 3:13, "Happy is the man *that* findeth wisdom, and the man *that* getteth understanding." Psalm 111:10, "The fear of the LORD is the beginning of wisdom; a good understanding have all they that do *HIS commandments* HIS praise endureth forever." Ecclesiastes 2:26, "For *GOD* giveth to a man that is good in HIS sight wisdom, and knowledge, and joy: but to the sinner HE giveth travail, to gather and to heap up, that he may give to *him that* is good before GOD..."

Colossians 3:16, "Let the word of CHRIST dwell in you richly in all wisdom; teaching and admonishing one another in psalms and hymns and spiritual songs, singing with grace in your hearts to the LORD." James 1:5, "If any of you lack wisdom, let him ask of GOD, that giveth to all *men* liberally, and upbraideth not; and **it shall be given him.**"

If you claim any of GOD's promises you must MEET THE CONDITIONS.

Made in the USA
Charleston, SC
14 November 2011